I'm Single...
and You're
About To Be,
Too

I'm Single... and You're About To Be, Too

Shunterria

MYND
MATTERS

Published by Mynd Matters Publishing
715 Peachtree Street NE
Suites 100 & 200
Atlanta, GA 30308
www.myndmatterspublishing.com

978-1-957092-13-3 (pbk)
978-1-957092-14-0 (hcv)
978-1-957092-15-7 (ebk)

FIRST EDITION

To my husband,
you were the catalyst for my transformation.

CONTENTS

INTRODUCTION

You either picked up this book for a little help or you picked it up because the title is catchy. Either way—WELCOME!

I will never forget attending the bridal shower of one of my best friends and hearing a married young lady tell my best friend that she should not take advice from single people. I know my face depicted all kinds of unladylike sentiments. I don't know if married folks think single individuals are just trash and not capable of keeping a man or maybe they think it is easy to find a good man. Whatever her reason was for that comment, I was utterly offended! If God can use a *donkey* to deliver a message, surely He can use my unmarried self to give wise advice to a person in need! Even if that person in need is married.

While I do *not* claim to be an expert, I am a woman who has heard the advice and complaints of husbands willing to be transparent enough to potentially stop me from making the same dreadful mistakes their partners have made. I appreciate their transparency because we live in a society where what goes on in the house, stays in the house. Now, I'm not saying tell *all* of your business. No, ma'am. However, I am saying know when to reach out and get help. It seems redundant to continuously suffer and go in circles when the world is full of resources we can use to better ourselves and improve our relationships. In full transparency, when I started writing this book, I was single. When I finished my final draft, I was one year and six months into marriage.

Therefore, know explicitly that I am *not* promoting divorce. Matter of fact, this book was written to promote the opposite, and to bring awareness to those oblivious partners and/or those who are in a difficult season in their marriage. The great news is you have the tools to maintain, enhance, or rebuild your marriage. When you and your spouse are willing to communicate, forgive, put in the work, and make necessary adjustments, you can have a fulfilling, successful marriage.

ONE

THE WOMAN IN THE MIRROR

So, you have been blessed with a man who is sensitive to your needs. He cooks for you as part of his contributions to your home. He notices when you have had a long, tiresome day, and he grabs your feet to massage them. (If you have *this* guy, you better praise God!) He genuinely enjoys serving you. Although he pays all of your bills, you find reasons to emasculate him. You talk down about the legit work he does and how he provides. Meanwhile, I'm over here drooling, waving my hand frantically wondering if he has a brother or a cousin who behaves similarly.

Not having the attitude of gratitude will earn you the quickest trip down Single Lane! As a Christian woman, it is HARD to be found by a Christian man *in* the church. Why? Because the men in the church are either already taken/married, gay, incompatible, or too darn old for your preference. You desire to be with a man who makes you feel beautiful, respected, cared for, and protected, but when you get that good man, how do you treat him?

How you treat your spouse is a reflection of you. It is said that some of us treat strangers better than we treat the people we love. Why is that? Brevity versus longevity? No expectations? Level of intimacy? I look at some wives and seriously wonder how they got their husbands. From their walk to their talk, they radiate nastiness, the kind that makes you not want to be in their presence for too long. "How do you wake up mad?" asked one of my frustrated male friends, in regard to his wife. It may seem funny for those on the outside, but to my friend, he was dealing with an extremely negative and moody partner. I'm not talking about being moody as a result of the constant hormonal changes women experience when it comes to that lovely time of the month. (For the record, that monthly chemical imbalance is real. I used to be in denial about my own mood changes during my menstrual cycles but now, I accept it for what it is and intentionally try not to be the extra butthole I could give myself the excuse to be.) I'm referring to the wives who have unpleasant attitudes on a daily basis just because.

Identity, Self-love, & Wholeness

Your behavior and attitude work together to compose your identity. Understanding your own identity is extremely important when connecting with another person. Identity plays a key role in your decision-making. It shows what you value and the principles by which you govern your life. With your own identity, you cannot be easily persuaded to do things that do not align with your morals. In a world of imitations, you value being your own self. You know who you are and that you belong to God. You are a daughter of the King.

Let's evaluate the importance of self-love. Self-love is not the same as being conceited, vain, or self-centered. Self-love requires a special kind of strength that advocates for yourself when you know you deserve better and can do better. It is a healthy sense of dignity and care for oneself. If you do not respect and care for yourself, how can you expect anyone else to? Self-love also includes possessing a healthy body image. There are plenty of women out here who are uncomfortable in their own skin. If you ask women to name the top three things they hate about their bodies, what do you think would be their responses? It would most likely include weight, unwanted body hairs, and the shape of our bodies.

Men are attracted to confidence. It took me a while to understand that, but it makes sense. Think about it. I'm sure you have witnessed unattractive men who acted like they were the "you-know-what." They were *confident!* Our men want to see us confident in the skin in which we were blessed to be encased. Hearing us constantly criticizing our bodies makes our men feel some type of way. It is an instant mood killer.

> *3 John 1:2 NKJV: "Beloved, I pray that you may prosper in all things and be in health, just as your soul prospers."*

If there are things we would like to change about our bodies, we have the power to do so. We cannot sit around all day and complain. We have to put in sincere effort to make the desired changes. Be conscious of how you treat your body. If we want to maintain good health, we must monitor what goes inside of our bodies. Everything we ingest affects our weight, our mood, and our energy or stamina. Push yourself to exercise regularly in order to increase your heart health. I encourage women to get involved in some type of regular physical activity that increases flexibility. This activity or routine can be as simple as stretching every day for ten minutes. Stretch often to increase flexibility and to decrease stiffness or soreness after physical activity with your spouse. You will see the difference stretching makes when you are in those crazy positions during sex *(you can thank me later)*.

Wholeness can be a confusing concept, especially in a relationship. We are used to hearing, "He completes me," but if the "he" is not Jesus Christ, we have it all wrong. A man does not "complete" a woman, he complements her, and the only way a man can complement her is if she is whole. Wholeness refers to not depending on anyone or anything to "make you happy." It means having a healthy amount of self-love and being able to be the best version of yourself because you have healed, forgiven, and been freed to move on to greater things. Wholeness allows you to bring 100% and give 100% to the relationship in which you are committed.

Rate your self-love with 0 being nonexistent to 10 being you love everything about yourself. _____

Why did you rate your self-love as such?

_____

_____

_____

_____

_____

_____

_____

_____

_____

If you rated yourself as having little to no self-love, what can you do to improve your self-love?

_____

_____

_____

_____

_____

_____

_____

_____

_____

Galatians 5:22-23 describes characteristics believers in Christ should possess, calling those characteristics, *The Fruits of the Spirit*. After your moment of self-reflection, take some time to analyze these nine characteristics and determine your current rating in each. Expect to be stronger in some areas than others because you're human and not perfect.

You are fearfully and wonderfully made in the image of God, according to Psalm 139:13-14. While true, we all have room for self-improvement. Don't be intimidated by that statement, be motivated! Choose to be grateful and confident in the lady Christ has made you and is making you to be.

Digging Deeper

Insecurity is a conscience-eating, negative emotion that weakens trust in relationships and ultimately, destroys them. It is a choice. As women, we tend to get comfortable in our insecurities. We get undressed and ease into those negative thoughts like a soothing hot bath. We soak in the doubt, low self-esteem, and the other emotions that come along with it. I remember the day I decided to stop being insecure. It was December 12, 2018. I was tired of worrying about someone's allegiance to me. Life comes with enough issues. Why be with someone you cannot trust? I just refused to continue to be insecure, especially in a relationship where we were discussing marriage. I'm an amazing woman only through Christ's correction and divine power. I believe in my whole heart that the Holy Spirit will show me what I need to see and guide me to where I need to be. Jesus has my best interests at heart, so why should I be afraid? If my significant other recognizes me as an amazing woman as well, he will preserve and protect our relationship. I have no desire to control a man. If he is faithful to me, that will be solely because of his own personal commitment to Christ and his decision to be committed to me and only me. It will not be by coercion or obligation but by privilege and love. If a person wants to be faithful, he or she will be faithful. If a person wants to cheat, he or she will cheat. It's as simple as that. All you can do is pray and watch. Hopefully, your significant other sees and understands your value and will not compromise your future together.

Sometimes, you may have unhealed and just plain rude thoughts in your heart towards your husband. I believe it is safe to say we *all* have been hurt to some degree or another. Too often we hold on to being mistreated by past boyfriends or ex-husbands. Then, we project those negative emotions onto our current mate. Some of us are even battling negativity that was spoken into our lives by our parents. If you choose to continue to carry that baggage, you will not be able to fly. Expose your hurt. That can be the hardest step, especially if you have purposely buried it within for a long time. Go to someone who can help you deal with the issue(s). I suggest praying about it first. Then, take guidance from the Holy Spirit. If you feel you need professional help, seek such services. We are meant to live *interdependently*; we are not meant to handle everything on our own. Pray for your own healing. Pray for your heart toward your husband. Ask God to clean and purify your heart and thoughts toward him and help you to see the best in him.

What are your thoughts toward/of your husband?

_____

_____

_____

_____

_____

_____

_____

_____

_____

If any thoughts are negative, how can you change those thoughts?

_____

_____

_____

_____

_____

_____

_____

_____

_____

Maybe the wife described above is you, but it does not *have* to be you. Your transformation can begin when you acknowledge how you treat your husband.

Do you remember the old saying: "You can catch more flies with honey than manure"? Well, it's test time! Has your *attitude* been honey or manure? Have your *words* been honey or manure? What about your *actions*? Have they been real sweet or real funky? Be honey in your marriage, not manure. To be a powerful queen, you do not have to be the meanest lady in the room. Constantly being mean to your husband is unacceptable, and a step in the right direction would be to apologize. Then analyze what it was that caused you to start being so cold, hostile, bitter, and/or rude toward your husband in the first place. Was it a change in his employment status? Was it a change in his attitude? Did something traumatic happen that you have not properly dealt with? Whatever it is, you can get that girl you used to be back. You can regain your joy and peace and learn to smile again.

Relationships are supposed to change the people in them, preferably for the better. You tend to learn a lot about yourself within the confines of a relationship. On the rare occasions when pushed too far, you may not have known how you would react until your back was against the wall.

I learned from my most recent relationship that I tend to give a lot of myself. I did not initially think that was a bad thing, but as I saw my mate not giving as much as I felt I was giving, feelings of being unappreciated and taken for granted arose and problems surfaced. On the contrary, several years ago, a friendship showed me I was judgmental and self-righteous. Luckily, but unfortunately, something unspeakable happened in my life that threw me off of that high horse. Now, I'm able to approach really complicated situations with mercy toward the individuals involved. If you are unwilling to change, a relationship (and most definitely a marriage) may not be for you. When two people from different backgrounds, diverse cultures, with different preferences (and everything in between) unite in hopes of a future together, there will always be a time when both parties are challenged to change. Whether that change takes the form of the way they speak to their partner, their home habits and hygiene, and/or the way they deal with finances, an adjustment is inevitable.

Side note for Singles: Have you considered you may have to change some of your ways and habits once you become a wife? Are you willing to do that? If not, why did you accept his proposal?

_____

_____

_____

_____

_____

The Center

Your first commitment and responsibility as a woman
of Christ is to follow and serve Jesus. We cannot have
a God-ordained covenant without God. It does not
work to our benefit. If our relationship with God is not
in good standing, all other relationships are at risk of
failing because God teaches us how to develop and
maintain healthy relationships. No person will meet all
of your needs and expectations. Ever since the movie
Why Did I Get Married? emphasized the 80/20 Rule, I
think more singles and married individuals try to be
more reasonable and accepting of those quirky, and
sometimes, annoying characteristics of their potential
mate or current spouse. I believe God did this so we
would have less of a reason to put anyone before Him.

Since we are on the subject of not putting anyone
before God, fight for and plan for uninterrupted time
with Jesus. This may require you to get up 30-45
minutes earlier than anyone in your house, but it is

worth it! My spirit always feels lighter and stronger after I have been in the presence of Jesus. I can think clearer after our encounter. It tends to be easier to walk in the Spirit when you spend quality time with Jesus daily and consistently.

During your time of devotion, remember to communicate with God. Please do not underestimate the power of prayer. One of my spiritual mentors would always say, "Stay prayerful." If you are not prayerful now, being in a serious relationship or marriage will help you get there. I cannot count the times my prayers have begun with, "Jesus, help me!" or "Jesus, I can't do this" (This being the relationship). Be real in your prayer life. Christ appreciates transparency and authenticity when you are meeting with Him. Though He already knows the situation, have that dialogue with Him. Jesus works in miraculous ways and His timing is just that—His timing.

It is imperative you find a mate who believes and practices the same spiritual values as you. You are walking together, so you need to agree on foundational principles such as that. If he loves you as Christ loves the church, then you are off to a great start. Your spouse should understand your TOP priority is your commitment to Jesus. Your spouse is your second priority. When you both put Jesus first, it is easier to be on one accord. I promise you will lean on God more in your marriage than you ever believed. Living with and committing to the same person takes supernatural power! Make it a priority to engage in godly activities together, such as prayer, devotions, fasting, and attending worship services. Do not count on him to lead everything. This can be unrealistic at times. After all, you are better and stronger in some areas. We see this a lot in spiritual areas. Wives tend to be more mature. You may have to initiate or lead prayer in your home. Try not to condemn him for this. We win our husbands through showing them the love of Christ, not condemnation.

Let the Holy Spirit do His job! Listen to the Holy Spirit when He tells you to "Be quiet" or "Be quiet!" The Holy Spirit gives us wisdom if we choose to accept it. LISTEN to Him. God can convict and correct more things in our silence than we can with our words of disapproval and rebuke. We cannot nag men into spiritual truths. We can only show them what the Lord shows us with truth in love.

The S-word

Society has twisted the concept of *submission* into a caveman theory that means a wife is to do whatever her husband says with no thought or rebuttal following his statement. Submission, in woman-friendly terms, is giving your husband the permission/privilege to take care of you. Submission is not only an act of love, but an act of respect, trust, and humility.

Out of respect for Christ, we submit ourselves to our spouse. When we, as women, are not submitting to our husbands, we are out of line. Some may call me "old-fashioned," but call me what you please. There is a blessing in submitting to your husband, especially when your husband is following Christ. If your husband tells you to do anything that is not in alignment with your spiritual values, am I telling you to submit to his requests? Heavens, no! Again, I am encouraging submission to husbands who are submitting to God. I believe we women don't understand the benefit attached to giving our husbands the responsibility of taking care of us. It is primarily your husband's duty to cover you, to make sure you and your home do not lack in tangible and intangible necessities.

If you are like me, an extremely independent woman, my goal was to show a man I did not need him. Who knew being too independent will have you single? Humans have a need to be needed. Even *with* a husband, you may struggle with letting him have the privilege of providing for you and taking on major responsibilities. Sometimes, the fear of being disappointed keeps you stuck in the mentality of "I'll just do it myself." You did <u>not</u> get married to just do it yourself! If you have to constantly remind yourself that you are not alone, do so. As talented and strong-willed as some of us are, we cannot do our parts and theirs, too. Let that man help you. He takes pride in providing for his lady.

Along with allowing your husband the privilege of taking care of his queen, you have to go into a relationship with the performance attitude that says: "You have been upgraded to the max when you got me!" Trust in your own value and know your self-worth. Know your man would be a FOOL to lose ALLLLL of that! I have made it my mission to out-beat my potential spouse/husband in my giving and serving. I never understood how we can give 100% on our jobs, but give the men we submitted and committed our lives to anything less than that.

Side note for Singles: Reflect on WHY you want to become a wife. Are there any qualities or behaviors in your potential spouse that, if not managed, could pose a real threat to your marriage? If so, pray on those things. Be honest with yourself and ask if you can see yourself in a healthy, happy marriage with those issues for the rest of your life.

What kind of wife are you now? (Be real, Sis)

_____

_____

_____

_____

_____

_____

_____

_____

What kind of wife do you desire to become?

_____

_____

_____

_____

_____

_____

_____

_____

_____

What would motivate you to become the wife you desire to be?

_____

_____

_____

_____

_____

_____

_____

_____

_____

_____

_____

Presenting Mrs.

I suggest wives make a vision board for their position as wife. A vision board serves as a physical reminder of what you are striving to accomplish. Include what you want your attitude towards your husband to resemble, goals you can independently work on to better your marriage, and how you want to see yourself in the future. Afterward, maybe you and your husband can create a vision board together.

Proverbs 29:18 (KJV): "Where there is no vision, the people perish: but he that keepeth the law, happy is he."

When people have a passion for their position, they tend to perform better. One piece of advice is to study for what you want to become. If you want to become a teacher, you have to study and practice in that role. If you want to become a fire fighter, you need to study and train with the equipment. The same thing should take place if you want to become a wife or a better wife. Study and apply what you learn. I hate to say this, but the simple reality is, not all women who are married are "wives." What I mean by this is a title does not determine your quality. Instead, the diligence, commitment, mannerisms, and knowledge you apply to that title are what matter. YOU make the title. If you do not enjoy being a wife, take the time to figure out why you do not enjoy this role. There could be an immediate resolution, but you will not know until you identify the issue.

A wife is a BLESSING and an asset, not a liability. I have always wanted to be the kind of wife that, once my husband found me, he would praise Jesus for me and all that God put in me and has made me to be. Be great in your marriage on purpose. Enjoy your position in your relationship. You are in an honorable position. Your husband chose YOU to do life with. ***Respect*** the position! You bring *favor* in his life and a crown to his head, not shame and rottenness (Proverbs 12:4). Be the queen of his heart and treat him like a king.

Two

EVERYBODY WANTS A PENIS, RIGHT?

Having a penis comes with responsibilities that some men are clearly not ready for yet. Yes, I blame society and its ridiculous double standards for the way "men" of this age behave.

The media, especially the music industry, glorifies men sleeping around, cheating, and doing whatever they please. It is time out for grown boys who think that sluttin' around and sowing wild oats in any ol' garden is acceptable. Society needs more Christ-like male role models who proclaim and display faithful husbands leading their families in a respectable way.

Three Ps

The role of a husband is not to be taken lightly. Men in these positions carry a lot of responsibility if they truly care about honoring this position.

Provision

We joke about the cave man dragging home some

animal he has slain for dinner, but men were created with the instinct to hunt (provide). Financial strains can cause uncertainty and frustrations to arise, especially for a man. When money is looking funny, husbands who take pride in providing begin to sweat. Besides any human-related loss, job loss is extremely difficult for a man to face. Be sensitive to the fact that your family's status is a reflection of your husband more than it is a reflection of you. When a man cannot take care of his wife and/or family, he feels like it is a reflection of him as a man. Therefore, he feels as though he has failed. Though we know a job or career does not make or define a person, that source and sense of provision and security is valuable to an honorable man's confidence and emotional wellbeing.

I can recall a particular situation that happened with a couple close to my mate. It was obvious that the wife was the dominating presence in their marriage. She walked in on a conversation about finances and found it appropriate to say something emasculating to her husband in front of his male friend. You could tell her comment was hurtful and downright embarrassing based on her husband's demeanor. Even if finances are not looking the best in your marriage *right now*, no husband wants to be put down about it, especially in front of another man. Actions like this will give the devil ammunition to use against a marriage. Your spouse needs to feel like he can make wise financial decisions regarding your home. To go a step further, he needs to feel that you trust the financial decisions he makes.

When a husband who enjoys and prides himself on providing reaches a low point, it is not the time to kick him while he is down. As his wife, he needs your encouraging words and support. You may need to increase your financial contributions with a *positive* attitude. Remind him that his authentic worth is found in his character and his walk with God. Tell him until he obtains a job or more income, you will make the necessary adjustments to maintain your home. Reassure him that you have his back! You are a team!

Though financial stability is imperative, there is more to provision than a couple of dollars in the bank. Consider if your husband provides you with a shoulder to cry or lean on. Does he lend a listening ear? Does he provide care, compassion, and encouragement when you are not your best? Is he a husband who offers support and celebrates you when you achieve important milestones in your life? Does he offer a safe environment that promotes effective communication, or does he see everything as criticisms and complaints? Is he a husband who becomes quickly defensive when you vocalize your thoughts and opinions?

Really examine these things and analyze what you both bring to the table. You may discover that your spouse is providing more than you give him credit for. I truly hope this is the case.

Conversely, you may see that your spouse is like millions of other men who think as long as the bills are paid, they have fulfilled their husbandly duties. A conversation needs to be had if your husband does not understand the areas where his level of provision could be increased to improve your marriage. Be gentle. I repeat, be gentle. You do not want to come off as being fault-finding, seeking to point out all the "negatives." This is one of those conversations that need to be had in love with an open heart with the sincere goal of strengthening your spouse and your marriage.

Protection

I had a hard time dealing with the "Where are you?" question. It felt intrusive at first until a boyfriend explained the importance of having someone know where I was in case anything happened to me. It's your spouse's responsibility to protect to you. They feel the weight of this delicate responsibility, especially in regard to you and your children. It may feel overwhelming if you did not have a fatherly figure who cared for you when you were growing up or if you did not experience that level of concern in any previous relationship. Either way, let him protect you. Men protect who and what they cherish with all their might.

Beyond physical protection, consider if he gives you emotional and spiritual protection. When a man cares for you, he does not want to see you hurt, especially if he is the cause of it. He is conscious of your emotional wellbeing and the people and things that alter it. He takes the time to constantly cover you in prayer. Let me be honest, to have a man who covers you spiritually is a rare gem. (If you have this kind of husband, I'm thanking God *for* you!) His emotional and spiritual protection helps to keep you internally grounded and fortified.

Problem resolution

Your personal repairman (your husband ☺) takes on projects as a problem solver because it is in his DNA. Even when you are not looking for a solution to a specific situation, his brain goes into problem-solving mode. I know, sometimes, you just want to vent to your husband and not hear his fix-all solution, so lovingly communicate that to him. This simple step can save both of you from possible frustration.

When things are not functioning properly in your home, his leading to create solutions is a blessing. For example, when the children get too crazy for you to handle, the strength in his presence should put the little gremlins in check. If the refrigerator is on the fritz or there are problems with the plumbing, he is the one creating the game plan for the next move. A good man wants his queen and his children to live comfortably in their home.

Passenger Side Driver

Men like to do things *their* way, without us micromanaging them. If your significant other is in the kitchen cooking breakfast or dinner for you, consider going in the living room or dining room if you don't think you can resist the urge to instruct him. Sometimes, we, as women, have to learn how to ride in the passenger seat. You can't drive from the passenger seat, so stop trying to control EVERYTHING!

I literally learned this concept in the passenger seat of a former boyfriend's car. Does he really have to drive home the way *you* want him to? I know you're independent. I know you are hard-working and headstrong (guilty). However, give your significant other or husband room to be the decision maker. We both know where we are going together. His way of getting there will not always align with your way of getting to the same destination. Does that mean either of you are wrong? No. I understand we all have preferences but let the man drive! Besides, the decisions we do not agree with ultimately falls on the shoulders of our husbands. If he is a great man, nine times out of ten, he has already considered the effects of his actions and its effect on you and your family.

Here are some questions to consider:

Am I/my family safe?

_____

_____

Does his way compromise our relationship with God?

_____

_____

_____

_____

What are the consequences of me just riding while we go his way?

_____

_____

_____

_____

_____

_____

_____

_____

_____

Do I trust his decisions? Why or why not?

_____

_____

_____

_____

_____

_____

_____

If I do not trust him enough to make wise, healthy decisions for me/ our family, why did I choose him?

_____

_____

_____

_____

_____

_____

_____

Honor his request even though you feel like there's a "better" way to do things.

Proverbs 16:18 "Pride goes before destruction, And a haughty spirit before a fall."

Humility is truly a virtue in any healthy relationship. I was once dating a man who was the epitome of pride and arrogance. His head was so far up his own butt, he could smell his intestines. Okay, maybe that was too graphic. He acted like he knew everything, and I mean everything. There was no correcting him without him putting down those individuals who knew what he apparently did not know at the time. Newsflash: Nobody wants to be with a know-it-all. It was like, *Dude, you know everything? EVERYTHING? Yeah...okay, miss me with that foolishness.* If you're involved with a person who cannot—let me rephrase that—who refuses to be corrected, taught, and/or acknowledge his mistake/apologize when he is wrong, you may want to reconsider things. No human being is always right. NONE. NOT ONE. Admitting that takes humility.

MY instinct was to knock him off that high horse with words that would embarrass and cut his ego into pieces. Then one day, the Lord put this into my spirit:

It was not my job to humble him;
it was His (the Lord's job).

I heard somewhere that a woman needs to cater to her man's ego. I never understood how important it was to also *protect* your man's ego until now. Ego sounds like a term of arrogance or cockiness, but it is a simple word for "confidence." Their "ego" is the headquarters for their feelings. Even the men who display macho and alpha dog attitudes have feelings. We have to let and make our husbands feel like men. A man needs to feel needed. A man needs to feel like the king in his home, respected and honored. A man needs to feel like he is the only one that can satisfy his woman. We cannot purposely destroy their egos if we want to remain the queens of their hearts.

Proverbs 31:26 (NKJV): "She opens her mouth
with wisdom, and on her tongue is the law of
kindness."

Husbands need to be mentally and emotionally poured into from their wives. They love to be praised! Wives have to learn how to show adoration and appreciation for their husband's work. There is no support like when YOU believe in your man. You should be his biggest cheerleader, so never let anyone cheer louder for him than you. Let him know you appreciate him. Try to be loving and encouraging as much as possible. Compliment him often and on purpose. I like to use a dry erase marker to write notes of encouragement to my husband on the bathroom mirror. Please do not compliment other people more than you compliment your spouse. This could mean the difference between creating a secure, confident spouse or someone who is always wondering, "Why doesn't she ever say anything good about me?" in the back of their mind. It is a great boost of confidence knowing your mate is pleased with you and proud of you. Speak to the king in him!

Being a Christ-like husband requires noble character, strength, and focus, so it behooves wives to spiritually cover their husbands with constant prayer. Intercede often, if not daily, on his behalf. Pray for peace and alertness in his mind. Pray for his heart, that it is always striving to reflect the heart of God and that anything not like Christ be purged from it. Pray for his weaknesses and insecurities, that the devil will not be able to use them against him to cause him to fall. Pray for his spirit, that it is in constant submission unto Christ and open for Christ to speak what he needs into it. Pray that your husband becomes all God created him to be. With so many things in the world that try to tempt him and discourage him, covering your husband in the spirit realm is a matter of life and death.

That's My Man!

Let's take a moment to be gracious toward the men in our lives and what they are required to deal with in this world. Women are human. Which means we are sometimes emotional, irrational, moody, talkative, hopeless romantics, broken, scarred, and a multitude of other things. Let me share something with you that opened my mind and changed my heart: "What you get is not always necessarily what you want, and what you want is not necessarily what you need." That will preach all by itself right there! Think about it. Some of us *need* husbands who will put their foot down and bring the thunder. Others need husbands who will soften our hearts. What we need does not always come in the form we <u>think</u> it should come. Medicine is a prime example. It may not taste good going down, but it works to heal beneath the surface.

Have you noticed any characteristics (good or bad) your
spouse exemplifies and wonder where they come from? If
so, ask him.

Don't forget to remember your husband's past. I did not say throw his past in his face. We must give grace to the past experiences and their effect on our partners. There are plenty of men who grew up without father figures. Some men have misinterpretations of what a man is "supposed" to do and how he is "supposed" to do it. Some men have been sexually abused at early ages and have not properly dealt with that pain. His experiences may have molded him into a rough-around-the-edges kind of guy, but Christ can put him back on the potter's wheel. You may have to love those perfect imperfections and hurts out of him. Be gracious. Win those small battles with and through the love of Jesus. You married your husband because you saw something valuable and great within him. Reflect on those qualities often.

THREE

HOME IS WHERE THE HEART IS

When your hunny steps through the door of your home, how do you greet him? Is it with a long to-do list? Is it with grumbling and complaining about the kids or work? Is it with a warm embrace and a kiss? Is it with a simple, "Hey, baby!" I can tell you right now, no man wants to come home every day to the first two.

It can be challenging to attentively listen to you upon his arrival when he has been dealing with business obligations for the past eight plus hours, then come home to a bombardment of more burdens. We have to give each other time to decompress from dealing with the world outside. Every once in a while, your hunny is going to have a not-so-good day, and that's okay. We cannot control the responses of our men when this happens, but we can give them the understanding and space to work out their frustrations without judgment. Being the emotional creatures we are, sometimes we make everything about us. However, we have to get to a point where we realize everything is not about us. We must be patient with our spouses when they are having a bad day. Offer him grace, sweet lady. Give him room to breathe and a safe place to vent. Don't forget comfort goes both ways, so comfort your man when he shows you he needs that gentle touch.

Does your husband dread coming home? If so, ask him why and write his response below. Reflect on it. If he doesn't, try to understand what makes it a positive experience for him and focus on maintaining what you have created with your spouse.

_____

_____

_____

_____

_____

_____

_____

_____

_____

_____

What can you do to change his response if it's a negative one?

_____

_____

_____

_____

_____

_____

_____

_____

_____

_____

What positive actions or words do/can you use to create a warm environment in your home?

_____

_____

_____

_____

_____

_____

_____

_____

_____

_____

Our attitude can change the whole atmosphere in a positive or negative way. Negativity is contagious, but so is positivity. Have some good, positive energy to share with your husband. We could have a whole conference on creating a warm environment in our homes. It is my goal to be a breath of fresh air to my spouse every time he enters our home. I like to meet my husband at the door and make him feel welcomed. Make him feel that you are excited to have his presence in your home. Home should be a refuge for you both. It should be that place where you can release your longest, deepest sigh of relief.

Song of Solomon 2:15: "Catch us the foxes, The little foxes that spoil the vines, For our vines have tender grapes."

Something I am learning is how to let my fiancé be comfortable in our home. For me, this meant not nagging about every little thing that is out of place. Sometimes, we (women) allow those little annoyances to cause tension in our marriages. An example I am staring at right now as I write these words are the two or three pieces of my fiancé's clothing that have been haphazardly placed in *front* of the laundry basket, instead of *in* the laundry basket. I just don't get it. However, I told myself there are things he does that are more annoying, which I could use that energy toward addressing.

Another example is my fiancé and I have completely different morning routines. I am the one who likes to wake up in quietness. While lying there, I may silently pray and meditate on my thoughts or plans for the day, then get up and work my way into extra sounds. When he gets up, it is an immediate "go" for all things—TV, videos, music, social media, news, etc. For a while, it drove me insane. Learning to accommodate the other person takes understanding and consideration. It can be a quick fix if both parties are willing. Earphones brought some peace into our home after we discussed the issue. If he decides to listen to whatever with his earphones on blast, I simply ask him to consider going into another room, so he will not wake me.

Then, there is the unfinished honey-do list. Meeeerrrccy! From everything I've heard or read, men seem to operate on a different time schedule than we do. That same to-do list can extend untouched for weeks to months. At this point, we are either ready to handle it ourselves or pay someone to take care of it for us. Yet, we have to learn the virtue of waiting. For the pet peeves and annoyances we cannot let go, we have to address them in love. Making the choice not to complain about everything will promote an atmosphere of peace, relaxation, and freedom in your home.

How often do you complain?

_____

What do you complain about?

_____

_____

_____

_____

_____

_____

_____

_____

_____

_____

All Up in My Space…At Home

One of my biggest adjustments was sharing my time with my mate…all the time. When my fiancé and I moved in together a month before our intended and planned wedding ceremony, that was a challenge. I'm an introvert who loves spending time with myself. Of course not in a narcissistic way, but I love the peace of just flowing how I wish. I could nap when I wanted. I could go to my favorite craft store as much as I wanted and stay as long as I wanted. I could have as many cereal meals as I saw fit. Well, as you know, all of those I's turn into we's when you decide to marry. You share your true self and commit to considering your significant other's needs. A dear friend of mine told me how her husband liked her just *being* in the same room with him, no conversation needed. He just enjoyed her presence. At first, I didn't get it. However, men and women are wired differently. They can enjoy the physical presence of their wives without verbal interaction. Whereas, we tend to crave interaction that is more emotionally engaging via verbal exchange. It's definitely an adjustment, right? Living together is a major transition where you learn how to compromise space and time as you strive to live in harmony.

Even married individuals need their personal space, at times, within their home. It is okay for each of you to have some "me-time" to relax on purpose. Personally, whatever I do in the bathroom is MY business. My man does not need to know what I am doing or visit me while I'm in the bathroom. That's my private time. The same is not true for all women though, and that's fine. If you do not mind your husband in the bathroom while you poop or pluck, that's your prerogative. However, the need for personal space is why someone created the "man cave" and "she-shed." These areas give us a space to decompress and relax, when needed. These areas also allow us to take a brief break from the various roles we play throughout the day or week. In the man cave, men can be just that—men. They can enjoy the loud noises, the ridiculous movies, food crumbs being everywhere without a word from their dear hearts. In your she-shed, you can take a moment for self-care after a rough day or even better, a day that Mother Nature has decided to unleash the beast on all of your lower organs during your cycle. In your she-shed, you can *savor* your favorite hidden snack. I'm talking about the snack you AND your husband like that you rarely get to enjoy, because some men just do not understand the concept of moderation. Don't judge me. Sometimes you have to hide your snacks to ensure the peace of your household! I call this being proactive about those things you know you have the tendency to nut up about that you actually *can* control. It is my hope that you have a space in your home where you can take a timeout and experience the comfort in the simple things if but for a moment.

Time apart outside of the home is healthy for the relationship when it is done in a respectful way. I love attending women's retreats out of town. They present the opportunities to escape to a different scene and be around a group of like-minded women who share a common interest in evolving into better women. Likewise, enjoying a girls' night with my sister circle (my best friends) is refreshing to my spirit. This presents time to indulge in girl talk and delve into issues that may be burdening our hearts. In addition to enjoying a refreshing night out with my girlfriends, I have the opportunity to miss my husband. Soon enough, I am ready to get back home to my man and get a little freaky.

> ***Proverbs 14:1: "The wise woman builds her house, But the foolish pulls it down with her hands."***

It is important to understand that, although women tend to manage the home ("run" is such a strong word), men folk should *feel* in control. Allowing them to feel in control does not mean ladies must take on every task in the home. Matter of fact, take note that you are not the only person following the expectations established for your home and relationship, and vice versa. Please make sure you are doing *your* part— honestly, that is all you can do. Do not be upset when your husband holds you accountable for your actions or lack thereof, as he should. Some wives do not take being confronted about their shortcomings to fulfill whatever expectations have been set too well. Meanwhile, they can point out everything their husband *said* they would do but did not get done.

Sharing household chores and responsibilities prevent both husband and wife from burnout, especially if you both work full-time. Just like a wife does not want a lazy husband, a husband does not want a lazy wife. Hold each other accountable for completing chores and projects. You are a TEAM. This means everyone must fulfill their role. Honestly, *basic* consideration goes a long way in any successful marriage. Actions as simple as asking your spouse, "Do you need anything?" while on your way home or washing the dishes after your spouse has prepared dinner for your home, can make a good relationship an even better one.

While briefly mentioning dinner, take care of your man. This includes monitoring his nutritional health as well. If you know your man is a diabetic, reconsider feeding him meals high in sugars and carbohydrates. Moderation has always been important, but if he cannot seem to be able to control himself, help him. You may have to take it a step further and personally sacrifice your own food choices to support his new eating habits. Maybe for your household this means buying less cookies, sodas, and chips and instead buying more fruits and fresh vegetables.

Something else I've noticed is the priority of individuals in a marriage. I have seen it from both sides—wives who put the church, friends, and children before their husbands and husbands who put business and their friends before their wives. This imbalance can cause friction between spouses and feelings of unimportance in the spouse who is always put on the back burner. I love when people ask me to do things. It tells me that should I accept their invitation, they believe in me to get the job done with a spirit of excellence. With that being said, don't bite off more than you can chew, even with church ministries. Some of us make the mistake of viewing the church as God himself, so when hearing the statement "Your husband comes before the church," we misinterpret it to mean "Your husband comes before God." This is not accurate, and it is imperative for you to realize the difference. Do not allow the number of ministries you are in to be the determining factor for your relationship with the Lord. So you're a woman of God in six different ministries, and you're married, and you work a full-time job? Out of those multiple things that require your time and effort, in at least one area, you're more than likely dropping the ball. Figure out which ministries God has actually called you to do, then prioritize. God is the God of order. He is a God of covenant. He does not desire for your marriage to fail. Having a spouse is a full-time job in itself! You are HUMAN. There's only twenty-four hours in a day (eight of which you are supposed to be sleeping).

It may come as a shock, but your husband comes

before your children. A healthy two-parent home does not only consist of mom and dad living together, but it is where the children can clearly see the love and respect mom and dad have for each other in a nurturing environment. Reach out and build a trustworthy support team. You need a family member or friend you can ask to babysit in order to put time and energy into yourselves and your husbands. There is no shame or judgment in regularly scheduling time to focus on your marriage after you add children to your family.

What helped me change my view about the order in which I prioritized things is recognizing that when everything else fades away or moves away (jobs, friends, children, money, etc.), I still have a commitment to take care of my husband and vice versa. I would rather be taken care of by someone who knows and has seen through my actions that I made him a priority.

When women feel like we are the top priority in the relationship, we naturally perform better. We are more supportive, more prone to initiate and be more physically intimate, and in general, more pleasant to be around. When we feel taken for granted and underappreciated, our emotional satisfaction decreases followed by a decrease in our home/wifely duties. I'm not saying it is right, but it happens. Happy spouse, happy house!

Everything that glitters isn't gold.

One of the top relationship killers is comparison. Comparing your current mate to your old "beau" is almost second nature. Although it is natural and feels innocent, it is not healthy or beneficial because the constant internal competition burdens your heart and clutters your mind. Figure out where your heart is and cut off old soul ties. Do not expect two different men to do the same things you like, unless you have clearly communicated your needs and wants to both of them in the same way. You may have to teach your mate how you prefer to be treated.

How do you want to be treated?

_____

_____

_____

_____

_____

_____

_____

_____

_____

This next statement has the potential to transform someone's marriage—here and now. Stop trying to emulate marriages you see. (Go ahead and take a minute to just shake your head.) You have a different spouse, and you are a different wife. It is helpful to adopt some principles and practices here and there from others, but make them your own in your own way. The same loud and aggressive demeanor that one wife may use to approach her husband may be too overwhelming for a husband who has a calmer, more easygoing nature. Healthy, successful marriages are not built overnight, so do not be fooled by the cute social media pictures. Marriages take a whole lot of prayer, grace, forgiveness, commitment, and love to get to that place where you are overall satisfied with your spouse.

Are you envious of another couple? If yes, why?

_____

_____

_____

_____

_____

_____

_____

_____

_____

_____

We cannot be involved in everybody's business and effectively take care of our own. Staying in others' business is different than helping. One way to distinguish the two is to ask yourself, "Was my input asked or mutually understood and consented?" Also, determine if you are being overbearing. It is in our genetic makeup to care for others. However, there is a line we need to be mindful of that we do not cross. When we lose focus of our own household matters, our performance gets weaker and potentially harmful things that we would not usually overlook, can slide through the cracks.

What is your level of involvement in other folks' business?

_____

Where (in **your** household) can you direct that extra time and energy?

_____

_____

_____

_____

_____

_____

_____

_____

A helpful thing to remember is: Make the most of what YOU have. Life is constantly changing. Some days, all of our needs and wants will be fulfilled. Other days, just our needs for the day will be satisfied. When my fiancé and I first got our apartment, we didn't have a dining table. We ate in the living room, sitting on our couch or in the dining room at the foldout table we used for vending events. It took time and effort to search for the dining set we wanted. Once found, we put a plan in place to obtain it. When we got our dining set, we moved onto the next items we wanted to attain. Bit by bit, with patience, we turned our bare minimum apartment into a more comfortable home.

It's the same with your marriage. You cannot expect everything to be miraculously perfected at once. You have to be patient. I think wives must remember what you see is not always what you get. Work and love must be put into the people we want to maintain a relationship with. Relationships change people, for the better or worse. Hold on to your spouse and stay encouraged. Be careful not to compare or covet another person's spouse or their belongings. It is amazing how much we can change our life by simply changing our perspective and remaining grateful for our spouse and circumstances. No spouse becomes perfect overnight. Continue to trust God and pray for your spouse as you partner with God to work on evolving into a better you. Appreciate your own marriage and put in the work to improve it where necessary to make your home one of flourishing love.

FOUR

A HOUSE DIVIDED

Matthew 12:25 (NKJV): "But Jesus knew their thoughts, and said to them: 'Every kingdom divided against itself is brought to desolation, and every city or house divided against itself will not stand.'

The devil's main tactic for destroying marriages is *division*. It does not sound like a deep revelation, right? He attempts to cause division in multiple ways, not limited to infidelity, such as financial strains, lies, dangerous habits, anger, being unforgiving, selfishness, and so many other ungodlike characteristics and actions. If it is not any of the examples listed, the devil will throw a different fiery dart (Ephesians 6:16) at your marriage in an attempt to separate you and your spouse. One of my more seasoned married friends advised me to realize the occasional mean spirit within my husband (fiancé at the time) is not him, but it is of the devil to cause division. Once you and your husband married, your strength was established in Christ and in sticking together. It is hard to win a battle when you are fighting against your own "battle buddy" (your husband).

Family can also play a huge role in creating tension between you and your husband. As a married couple, no one is to come between you two—not parents, not even kids. There are instances where one spouse's mother causes tension between the husband and wife. This should not happen. A respectful honor and reverence is due to our parents. However, parents should not be put before your spouse. I am not referring to those special cases where one of your parents is in need of frequent care for health reasons. I mean in everyday marital matters, the spouse's parents should not have so much influence that they are habitually interfering. You know those parents who are constantly in your household's business and inserting their unwarranted opinions and negativity. No, ma'am, Pam. Discuss this with your spouse (if it has not already come up) and decide how to approach the situation. Respectfully address the parent and be firm on your position and the boundaries of YOUR marriage.

As for other members of the family, do not allow your children to play you and your husband against each other. This goes for step-children as well. Playing parents against each other can include acts like going to the other parent when one parent has said no. You both should be a united front, operating as one unit sharing the privilege of rearing them.

You must also operate as a united front in the presence of specific family members that have demonstrated immaturity or disrespect toward you and/or your relationships in the past. You may have to school your husband on their personalities and ill spirit, so he can stay away from them on purpose. Misery loves company, and that is not the kind of company either one of you should desire keeping.

You Stay on Your Phone!
Phones are a daily necessity for existing in modern society, but they have their respective places in relationships. Just when we thought people could actually be involved in face-to-face interactive relationships, social media crept in and sucked the life out of them. What happened to the days when couples had each other's undivided attention? What happened to the time when notifications and dings from Facebook, Instagram, and Snapchat were not fighting for its share of quality time? The time when pictures and check-ins were not required for a person to feel like they were "living their best life?"

Don't lose your life looking at everyone else living theirs.

I've never been a person to blast my personal life on social media. To me, this just gives people the ammunition to hate and talk about something they don't truly know about. I have experienced instances when I have tried to let the world in on a small piece of my life, only to have people comment, showcasing their jealousy and thirstiness. There have been instances where an inside joke between friends was misinterpreted by family members and God only knows who else. If innocent banter has caused eyebrows to raise, what do you think flat-out public disputes among spouses can cause? We must consider the content we post on social media as married individuals.

Your personal phone holds a hidden key that opens the private treasure box of you. The contents of your phone tell depths about who you are, what you enjoy, what your dreams and ambitions are, and even your deepest secrets. Both spouses have a responsibility to provide security in the relationship. If your mate has to fight with your phone for your attention, you are not providing security or quality time. If you're on your cell phone at all times of the night, it attracts suspicion, and is straight-up disrespectful. Don't hold your phone more than you hold your mate. Having that open access to each other's phone can break down the walls of insecurity. It is not necessarily giving up your privacy as much as it is showing your spouse you have nothing to hide. Not every relationship requires this amount of openness. However, if it does, I pray you and your spouse have a marriage worth more than the contents of your device.

Let's Get Ready to Rumble!

> *Proverbs 21:9 (NKJV): "Better to dwell in a corner of a housetop, than in a house shared with a contentious woman."*

Did you and your spouse argue about making the bed, now you are ready to leave him? Has he still not completed the one or two household chores you asked him to do almost two weeks ago?

If so, honey, breathe.

I can laugh now because I have been there and done that. Where is the "there" and what is the "that" you may wonder. The stupid fights couples have over the most minute things. It was a challenge to continue staying in our home, especially after arguments. Before, we could argue then one of us could leave and go to our respective home. After moving in together, we would argue. Then I would think, "I wish you would go home," but he was already home. What a trying time that was!

When our expectations are not being met, arguments and/or conflicts are usually the byproduct. It is okay to have expectations, but the challenging part is determining whether or not your expectations are realistic. It is not okay to assume your mate should already know your expectations, even if he was previously married or in serious relationships before you. Make time to vocalize your expectations and express your concerns with your partner. For example, your husband may expect to have sex twice a day, every day of the week. While it may be possible, you must consider the external factors of children (if you have any), work, household responsibilities, etc. You, on the other hand, may only want to have sex three times a week, because of the aforementioned factors. With communication, you two should be able to reach a compromise that may require a little sacrifice on both ends, but those expectations should be clearly defined.

What are your relationship concerns?

_____

_____

_____

Another cause for tension to manifest is when one or both spouses are going through internal conflict, anything that disturbs your peace and creates a state of unrest in your heart. Internal conflict can take the form of health concerns, spiritual questions, childhood traumas, etc. The length of time you or your spouse may experience this depends on any extenuating circumstances that surround the issue. It typically consumes a lot of your mental and emotional energy as you contemplate ways to change the situation or how to change your feelings about the situation. One personal example was my desire to transition into a new career. I have worked in education for slightly more than ten years, but my passion for it faded. Mind you, I have a master's degree, and even with that, it was difficult to find another job that compensated equally or more than the position I occupied. I felt I had wasted three years of my life in school preparing for a career that did not seem worth the energy. This was more than frustrating, it was downright discouraging. Not to mention the student loan debt that accompanied my attempt to develop professionally. Oh, do not let me forget the icing on the cake. We were smackdab in the middle of the worldwide coronavirus pandemic. This internal conflict and outward attempt at finding another job caused a bit of strife between my husband and me. It's amazing how things seem so easy to the "outside-looking-in" people. What I learned was not let other people's lack of understanding, their timeline, and their personal opinion of *your* purpose hinder you from finding or following *your* passions and purpose. Dealing with my own thoughts and feelings in this period were already draining enough, but being mindful of my husband's feelings toward my attempt at transitioning left me feeling unsupported and alone.

After verbalizing things with each other regarding the dynamic, he began to show more empathy and support. In a lot of ways, he had experienced a similar situation, but his recollection of his transition was blinded by his elevated position. In plain words, he forgot where he came from.

At some point in time, you will take turns bearing each other's burden. Even when you experience difficult times, continue to make yourself accessible. When we are going through hard or chaotic situations, one of our first instincts tends to cause us to withdraw or disconnect. The Bible declares that, when a man isolates himself, he seeks his own desire and rages against all wise judgment (Proverb 18:1). It sucks going through trials as a couple. However, there is comfort in knowing you have someone to face trials with. Maybe this is one reason God said it is not good for man to be alone. We are to be helpmates to those delicate creatures called "husbands." We should come equipped with wisdom to share, strength to support, and love to build them up. It is definitely no easy task, but it is one that is humbling. It has the potential to reap many rewards if we serve our husbands as though we are serving Jesus. We committed to share our lives and that includes the difficult times as well. Open up and let each other into that conflicted and emotional space. Listen with compassion and listen to understand.

What are you and/or your spouse having a hard time dealing with right now? _____

_____

_____

How can you or your spouse be sensitive towards this issue?

_____

_____

_____

_____

_____

_____

_____

_____

That's a NO for me

You may not want to hear this but conflict grows you as a unit. It challenges your character to be strengthened in various areas. The key is learning how to handle conflict and disagreements when they arise, because they are inevitable. However, respect should not be an option. Also, whether we want to recognize it or not, your husband is the answer to your problem (because he IS the problem). Fix those eyebrows and give me a chance to explain. Your husband is the best person to consult with when attempting to solve a problem related to him. He is the best person to explain his feelings, opinions, and perspectives. He is also the person you are looking to for a solution that will ultimately require some sort of action on his part.

It can be difficult to be reasonable when intense emotions are in the mix. Establishing boundaries for arguments remind both people to be accountable for their actions, even in an intense moment. One husband

I spoke with said he told his wife that leaving the house and staying out overnight after an argument is a problem. He told her that, if it happened again, once she returned, he would not be there and neither would his belongings. That whole leaving the house and your mate not knowing where you are going is a big no-no. It is a surefire way to add fuel to the fire. While accomplishing your goal of pissing off your mate, be mindful that space and time create room for insecurities to fester. While it is a possibility that the absent mate is not doing anything suspect or extramarital, are those the games you want played in your relationship? Unfortunately, it takes little to no effort for people to seek revenge, and when the shoe is on the other foot, stuff gets "real" really fast.

Moment of Reflection
Are you the reason for most or all of the arguments in your relationship? Be honest with yourself: _____

_____

Outside of infidelity, what are some of the main reasons for your arguments? (insecurity, physical factors (hungry, tired, in pain), finances, or something else?)

_____

_____

_____

_____

_____

How do you handle your anger?

_____

_____

_____

_____

_____

_____

_____

_____

Know your limits and know your spouse's limits, too. Everyone has a point where enough is enough. An essential part of getting to know your spouse is discussing triggers that escalate conflict between you. Understanding each other's triggers help you maintain healthy boundaries during disagreements. Knowing his points of irritability will help you be a tad more gracious toward him. There is a time and place for everything. Recognize when to hit pause in a heated situation. Disagreements should not be happening in front of family, friends, and the general public. It should never be your goal to embarrass your partner in front of anyone. Even if you decide to leave your home for a few moments in order to cool down, please choose to put on or keep your wedding ring(s) on your finger and communicate where you are going.

What are some ways you can calm down during heated moments?

_____

_____

_____

_____

_____

_____

_____

_____

_____

Watch your intentions during conflict. Really analyze the goal of your actions and words. Do you want the truth? Do you want to resolve things? Do you just want to hurt your partner? Name-calling during a disagreement is unacceptable, and neither is physical abuse. It is hard to forget the vicious, hurtful words said during an argument, even when the argument is over.

Another difficult thing to forget is when your spouse constantly brings up past issues and uses them as arsenal during a disagreement. I would use my fiancé's previous divorce as a tool of hurt and a reminder of his "failure." The Lord convicted me of this and told me to stop bringing up my mate's previous divorce in arguments. Obeying this instruction from the Lord was a game-changer for my heart and my intentions during conflict with someone who I intended to love, honor, and cherish for the rest of my life.

How would your relationship with your husband change if you really believed, "When I hurt my husband, I hurt myself?"

_____

_____

_____

_____

_____

_____

_____

_____

_____

_____

Proverbs 15:1 (NKJV): "A soft answer turns away wrath, But a harsh word stirs up anger."

For decades, the stereotype has been established that women love to talk. Now, I will neither confirm nor deny that, but most of the women I know (and love) can talk the horns off a goat! With that being said, ladies, everything that comes in your mind does not need to come out of your mouth. It's as simple as that.

Being "real" is not about saying what you want, when and how you want. This is immature and reckless. Words really do scar people. A lot of people enjoy sarcasm, using it as witty banter. While they may not mean any harm by it, others may perceive those remarks as hurtful and rude, leaving its receivers feeling disrespected and demeaned. It would be in our best interests to take inventory and determine if sarcasm in any given situation would create a laughable moment or a negative response. We do not want our sarcastic remarks to escalate an already heated situation.

Speaking the truth in love can be challenging when emotions take over. However, we must learn to weigh our words. Take the time to *process* what you want to say before responding to your spouse (or to anyone). In doing so, you are allowing yourself to play back the words (in your head), and internally hear what type of message your words may be conveying. When we are at odds with our husbands, it is easy to not see them as the men we care for and love. They become the enemy, the opposer, the one we have to protect ourselves from. When you remember you and your husband are on the same team, it makes you more conscious of the way and reason you say what you say.

It is easy to forget that communication does not only consist of the words we say and the tones we use, but it involves our body language and our facial expressions. The previously mentioned nonverbal cues make up about 55 percent of the messages we relay. Based on this information, ask yourself: "What is my facing saying?" I have been told on multiple occasions to "fix my face" because my face tends to tell what I am thinking before words leave my mouth. If you are like me, you may need to make it an intentional goal to practice your responses both verbally and physically.

One thing that has struck me while in the process of learning how to communicate with my now-husband is that we really wanted the same thing, but we verbalized it in different ways. It is sad that relationships end because people refuse to explain and/or understand the message behind the words. This is where communication and transparency can further shift the relationship. Your husband should be able to talk to you about anything and vice versa. I understand that some topics are harder to address than others, but you want to create an environment of safety, trust, and understanding for when those conversations arise. Transparency in relationships offers a new level of respect and requires maturity. Sometimes if you want to go deeper and get answers to nerve-racking questions, you have to prepare your mind and ears for something you may not want to hear.

Arguments with no solution make me feel like the argument was in vain and a plain waste of energy. Ask yourself: "Is the problem over or has it been resolved?" These are two different results. When a problem or heated discussion is over, the conversation ceases. However, when a problem has been resolved, a course of action is established to prevent future complications. Try to avoid bringing up past disagreements with no relevance to the current issue. Keep in mind to remain solution-oriented, meaning, be ready to create and discuss possible solutions to the conflict at-hand. Do not be afraid to admit if you made a mistake. If you feel like you and your husband need a mediator to help in the process of creating resolutions, invest in your marriage. Do not let shame and pride prevent you from seeking assistance.

It is not wise to throw the d-word (divorce) around

carelessly. That is a serious threat to your marriage. The devil will use that to attack you and your husband at your very core. Words give life to our thoughts and emotions. Strive to make divorce a non-option. Take it one day at a time. Choose to reflect on better times and focus on positive things. Speak life into your relationship. You have invested time into your partner, time you can never get back. Do not give up if it is worth fighting for. Every time you go to your husband in respect and love, you fight for your marriage. When you listen to understand, you fight for your marriage. When you give grace when it is tempting to read him like your favorite book, you are fighting for your marriage.

> *Ephesians 4:32 (NKJV): "And be kind to one another, tenderhearted, forgiving one another, even as God in Christ forgave you."*

> *Colossians 3:12-13 states, "Since God chose you to be the holy people he loves, you must clothe yourselves with tenderhearted mercy, kindness, humility, gentleness, and patience. Make allowance for each other's faults, and forgive anyone who offends you. Remember, the Lord forgave you, so you must forgive others."*

Typically, after a disagreement, we refuse to serve our spouse. We stop cooking. We stop doing his laundry. We stop engaging in sex with him. I understand the reasons, of course, because I am a woman. Let us verbally expose those reasons together. Some women use the withholding of sex as a form of "punishment." When you withhold sex from your husband, you give the devil a foot in the door to lure either or both of you with physical or sexual temptation. There are other women who have withheld sex from their husbands because they were angry or hurt. When emotions are in that state, it is hard for the female physical body to align with reactions that prepare it for a sexual experience. To make it clearer, if a wife is upset with her husband, her vagina typically does not scream, "Come hither!" To conquer those negative emotions that women feel, peace needs to be achieved between the husband and wife. It is highly possible that makeup sex will follow the act of peace and forgiveness, especially if there has been tension between the two for days. I do not know exactly what it is about makeup sex that makes it so satisfying but whew!

It is hard to take the highroad when we feel wronged in the situation. Why do we think the silent treatment is effective? Days go by as we keep our anger and frustration bottled up inside while fighting to complete our daily tasks and maintain our sanity. Along with the silent treatment, holding grudges has proven to be ineffective as well. Sometimes, we face situations where we want to move on from a mistake our spouse has made, but the victim mentality inside of us does not want to let it go. Sometimes, we feel it is our right to remain upset, even when our spouse is trying to settle things. We want a sincere apology, recognition of the wrong, and, at times, revenge. Revenge sounds so malicious, so we will call it "reciprocity." We have to process those emotions then communicate them effectively. Be humble. Put your stubbornness to the side for the sake of reconciling. Forgiveness is such a powerful tool. Forgive your spouse and allow him the grace to evolve into a better man.

There is no love without forgiveness. There is no love without grace. What do you need to let go of?

_____

_____

_____

_____

_____

_____

_____

_____

Stress brings out the wimps or the warriors in any relationship. I can recall dealing with high tension very early in my marriage. I was sitting in my favorite (only) rocking chair on a Thursday evening as it was approaching time for my church's online Bible study. The message was "Don't Faint!" with the key scripture deriving from Proverbs 24:10: "*If you faint in the day of adversity, your strength is small.*" I lost it. That was the moment when this particular scripture became a personal revelation for me. It hit my spirit with such an explosion of inspiration to hang in there. Yes, it may take a considerate amount of grace, patience, and strength, but you will look back and be proud of what you weathered together. The situation will almost always make you stronger together.

Truly understanding that neither one of you will always get it right should help alleviate some of the pressures of marriage. There will be days when you feel like you have no idea what you are doing. Then there are days when you have a sense of your footing and feel like you can baby step your way to the next moment. A marriage is a promise to GOD that regardless of how my spouse behaves, I will stay committed to him for life. That is one heck of a promise! However, maintaining the mindset that *no one is going anywhere* is one that will help you get through trying times. If you are like me and stay upset for days, remember time does not care who we are mad with and why. It just keeps on ticking and passing us by. Time is a valuable gift. We have to be careful how we choose to use it. Something that seems so big at one moment can lose its magnitude once tempers ease. I have rolled over to look in the face of my sleeping husband and thought, "This man gets on my everlasting nerves," but at the end of the day, we are still here—still standing, still committed, still growing in love.

Marriage is not for the faint of heart.

FIVE

TWO NICKELS TO RUB TOGETHER

I did not understand the depth of finances in a relationship until I started being more and more exposed to situations where I was using the money I had earned to benefit my partner. I knew financial sacrifices had the potential to happen at some point in any serious relationship because life happens. However, I thought I would be scripted in a fairytale where my mate would be the one sacrificing for me. You know the fantasy that the movies portray where the executive husband shells out hundreds of dollars for his wife's frivolous shopping habits? Well, my reality played out a little differently.

Before you go giving me the side-eye, "I ain't no gold digger!" I went off to college directly after high school. While attending classes, I worked part-time to handle the expenses of staying off campus. If I could go back in time and be taught anything as a teenager, I would have chosen financial literacy. Around my junior year, I got suckered into getting a credit card. The "buy now, pay later" arrangement gave me too much freedom as a naïve novice with credit. Upon graduating college, I was blessed to enter into the career I had attended college to prepare for. Years later, after paying off thousands of dollars in credit card debt plus my car loan, I had finally become financially stable. For me, this was a place where I felt I could save more without dipping into my savings after all my bills were paid. I felt accomplished! I felt FREE! Then the unthinkable happened. My fiancé lost his job.

This left me with the responsibility of taking on all the household bills. There was a sense of losing all I had built financially, yet I was still grateful that one of us had a job. It was not the insufficient income of my fiancé, but the question of whether my giving would be worth it. Not that I was trying to buy love, but the deep thoughts of "How will all my sacrificing end" arose in my mind. I remember being determined not to worry. I was ready to face the battle ahead. Let me add that Jesus was and is faithful. We did not lack for anything because He kept providing financial blessings for our household. Before I could contemplate a budget for the following month's bills, my fiancé gained employment with another company and reclaimed his place as the financial head of our household.

Side note for Singles: Start evaluating your financial status now, before getting into a serious relationship with someone. If it is not looking good, work on turning it around. It will require sacrifice, but it will be well worth it when you have a good financial status to add to what you are already bringing to the table.

There are individuals who go the distance in their jobs or careers until retirement. Others experience a season where a shift in their position or field needs to take place in order to increase their personal fulfillment. Once again, communication is key. The spouse desiring the career change may have to hang in said current position until the next move can be made. Most of us would stick it out, going to a job and getting a paycheck to support our family versus just quitting and hoping for the best. Enduring this process takes a huge amount of support from the other spouse. It is hard enough going to a job that you no longer have a passion to perform while dealing with negativity from an unsupportive spouse. In addition to that, the labor market is competitive and can be extremely discouraging when aiming for a new job or career change. Believe me, I know. God wants us to enjoy whatever honest work we perform (Ecclesiastes 5:18-19). Until the next opportunity arises, we must keep the faith, remain resilient, and make the adjustments needed to strive toward financial freedom.

Do your financial goals align?

Financial issues are one of the main reasons couples get divorced. Money is a valuable resource, but to think that a man and woman would break their covenant to God because of it makes me sad. I have witnessed firsthand a couple on the brink of divorce because of a husband's impatience with his wife's financial status at the time. He wanted her to be producing more, although she seemed to be producing equally at his level. If you can relate, gently help your husband to recognize your contributions to maintaining and even growing your household's income. It could simply be a moment where the pressures and pursuit of life clouded his reality.

Having a joint account can make finances easier and much harder, simultaneously. Some couples choose to put both individual and collaborative expenses and income together, thus having one account where everything is handled. Other couples choose to set up a joint account for home and collaborative expenses, and still have their individual personal accounts. This setup allows for a little independence in each of their spending without having to consult one another about every purchase. Speaking of which, it is a good habit to consult your spouse when large sums of money will be taken out of your joint account for big ticket purchases or loans. Surprises tend to be more exciting when money is *added* to your account, not taken away. There is no right or wrong way to go about this as long as you and your spouse are openly communicating and come to a mutual decision on how you wish to handle your financial matters.

You should be able to trust each other with finances. There are cases where one person lacks money management skills. When this happens, he or she needs to be able to openly communicate and even ask for help from the person with stronger money management skills. If you and your husband have a budget in place and a goal as to where that saved money is going, do your part. Control your spending. If you cannot afford to purchase a specific item or go somewhere luxurious when you want, try to remember it is just a sacrifice for your home's financial well-being. You cannot eat steak on a baloney budget. In other words, do not try to keep up with the Joneses. Do what is within *your* budget.

Try not to worry about what others around you think about how you may need to live temporarily in order to stabilize or maintain your house. Keep your eyes on your own pockets.

I do not believe people aim to be poor. With no direction or vision, it is easy to fall into a poverty or "just enough" mentality. You are striving to build a future together, and building takes work. List the debts that need to be resolved, then make a financial plan together. Some people like to tackle the smallest debt first, then work their way up to the largest debt. I like to tackle the debt with the largest interest rates and finance charges first. Whatever works for your home at the time, go that route. *Write the vision and make it plain* (Habakkuk 2:2). Your spouse should be the best accountability partner/inspiration you have when striving to become debt-free.

It is important for both of you to remember that plans do not always manifest accordingly. Life happens. A vehicle breaks down. Immediate family members die, and we may be responsible for giving them an appropriate burial. We help a friend in need. Be gracious toward your husband and yourself in this area as well. Situations like these have the potential to cause financial setbacks. Therefore, they can discourage us and leave us prey to fall into a downtrodden state.

Multiple streams of income can help provide additional resources to alleviate the stress of financial burdens. Once you and your husband handle the emergency, get back to the plan. If the plan needs tweaking, tweak it, and get back on track.

Moment of Reflection
What are your goals toward building financial security for your household?

_____

_____

_____

_____

_____

_____

_____

_____

_____

_____

What are your husband's goals toward building financial security for your household?

_____

_____

_____

_____

_____

_____

_____

_____

_____

_____

What are the necessary steps to achieve these goals? (I.e. credit repair, settling debts, tax resolution plans, etc.)

_____

_____

_____

_____

_____

_____

_____

_____

_____

How can you help each other accomplish your goals?

_____

_____

_____

_____

_____

_____

_____

_____

_____

_____

What other streams of income can you create for your financial freedom?

_____

_____

_____

_____

_____

_____

_____

_____

Matthew 6:21 (KJV): "For where your treasure is, there your heart will be also."

1 Timothy 6:10 (NKJV): "For the love of money is the root of all kinds of evil, for which some have strayed from the faith in their greediness, and pierced themselves through with many sorrows."

There is nothing wrong with desiring to be financially stable. We go wrong when we put working or obtaining money before our relationship with Christ and His will for our lives. When we regard money as THE source of our security, power, and value, we are idolizing money. Let's admit it. If some of us were wealthy, we would think we were all that and then some! In our prideful ignorance, we would behave as if we do not need God. We must recognize that God gives us the power to get wealth, according to Deuteronomy 8:18. Jesus wants us to prosper, and this is not limited to financial wealth. However, if that is what you desire and work toward, with the help of the Almighty God, you can achieve it. He is our ultimate source of provision (Jehovah Jireh), security, strength, and abundant life.

We are called to be good stewards of our income, but not to obsess over it. I'm not saying be complacent, but be *thankful* for where you are now. Utilize your gifts and passions to earn an income and let God handle the rest. Remember to tithe to your church home. "I would rather have a blessed 90 percent than a cursed 100 percent," a friend told me while we discussed tithing. We are to take care of God's house, and in turn, He will take care of our houses. He said, if He clothes the field and feeds the birds, will He not take care of you? (Matthew 6:26-34 NKJV).

Pray for Jesus to guide the financial decisions of your home. There are instances where a husband may be anxious and attempting to dabble in everything here and there for a chance to hit a lick (prosper). If something in your spirit is telling you that a specific financial move will not be in the best interest of your household, address your concerns with your husband in love and kindness. As a wife, continue to pray for your husband to move in wisdom, according to the Spirit of God. I really have a special place in my heart for wives whose husbands have an entrepreneurial spirit. These wives must have a higher level of resilience and encouragement to constantly offer their husbands in the midst of supporting them to accomplish their dreams. Sometimes life's circumstances gets in the way of progress, so remind your spouse of his dreams. Check in with him to get updated on his progress. We all need encouragement to reach our full potential. Surround yourself with people who can offer knowledge and encouragement when needed. Believe you can rise to all that God has put in you to live the abundant life!

Six

WHO YOU WITH?

We have heard the saying, "It takes a village to raise a child." Well, it also takes a village to support a healthy relationship. More specifically, it takes a village to support a healthy marriage. I remember the moments when I wanted to give up on my relationship, and the phone would ring. My momma was on the other end with words of encouragement, telling me to look at the bigger picture. She reminded me that the little issues would not be issues if we were living without the pressures of the worldwide pandemic we were dealing with at the time. "We have to have bad times in order to appreciate the good," my daddy said. Then he would always conclude with, "It's gonna be alright."

Examine your inner circle.

Who do you hang out with?

_____

_____

_____

_____

_____

Describe their character. Are they trustworthy? People
of integrity?

_____

_____

_____

_____

_____

_____

_____

_____

_____

Are they faithful to their mates/husbands?

_____

_____

_____

_____

_____

_____

How do they treat their spouse? Their family?

_____

_____

_____

_____

_____

_____

_____

_____

_____

What comprises the content of most of their conversations?

_____

_____

_____

_____

_____

_____

_____

_____

_____

Birds of a Feather

You must pay attention to this because your inner circle has a great impact on your character and actions. Am I saying not to go shopping with your favorite cousin who does not care about anybody and says what she wants when she wants? No. I am saying be aware of what she is feeding your mind and spirit. If a night out with the girls does not encourage you to be a better woman or, at least, provide the environment for you to maintain the respectful standards of your relationship, then maybe you're around the wrong group of companions. Build friendships with women of honorable character, especially women who are happily married, faithful women. Encourage your husband to do the same with happily married, faithful men.

You need a trusted friend who you can vent to about problems that you are experiencing in your marriage. Personally, I do not believe whoever you vent to has to be married to understand the issues burdening your heart and possibly offer you wise advice. I do believe that person has to love you and genuinely have your best interest at heart.

Speak well of your partner behind their back and make it a habit. We don't realize the power of our words and the weight words hold. Imagine having a friend who always speaks negatively about her partner, the person she has decided to dedicate her loyalty and time to, the same person she is supposed to edify. It is not a good look, especially to those predators who do not support or care for that relationship. Now, imagine a couple that constantly speaks well of each other, in and out of the other's presence. This creates solidarity and a sense of protection for your relationship.

You Married His Family, Too, Sis...

Many people become frustrated when thinking about congregating with their spouse's family. They do not want to engage in uncomfortable conversations or feel pressured to participate in things they do not prefer. They do not want to be in the toxic environments that serve as incubators for the next dramatic situation to occur. What do you do when you do not care to be around his family? You be cordial and respectful. You are not required to be BFFs with anyone in his family, but it is expected that everyone is to be respected. I have dealt with some interesting family members of previous boyfriends, and I will tell you right now it has not always been easy. I did not trust some of those family members because of their words and actions. Some were intrusive. Some were pushy and borderline controlling. It is the spirit of Christ in us that gives us the grace and wisdom to interact with those individuals. His spirit allows us to stand firm in truth and strength while defending us. His spirit gives us what to say and the love, yet boldness, to say it. As women of Christ, we can be bold, respectful, honest, and loving all at the same time.

Which of your man's family members or friends do you prefer not to associate with?

_____

_____

_____

_____

_____

_____

_____

Why?

_____

_____

_____

_____

_____

_____

_____

_____

How can you better deal with that person?

_____

_____

_____

_____

_____

_____

_____

_____

We Can't Be Friends

The controversy surrounding the question if men and women can *just* be friends has gone on for decades. It gets more complicated if both friends are married or if one of the friends is single and the other is married. The discussion came up one evening between my girls and me. The first question asked was, "What times of the day are respectful to contact a friend who is the opposite sex and married?" The consensus was between the hours of 10 AM and 9 PM, unless it was strictly business-related.

The next question was, "How frequently should the married and single friend communicate with each other?" Two of the five women involved in the discussion stated they would be curious as to what the conversation was about if it occurred every other day or daily. I added that I would watch his actions to see how said married person behaves when he or she is conversing with their single friend of the opposite sex?

I'm not saying be naïve or overlook tell-tale signs. If it is obvious something is not right, gather your evidence and address it. No one likes accusations without facts and examples. If your spouse is willing to change the behaviors that you are uncomfortable with, you know he values your relationship.

Both the husband and the wife have a *duty* to make each other feel secure. Creating insecurity in your relationship is a dangerous game. There's a special kind of admiration for people who are straight up and not interested in playing games that could damage their character or their relationship and home. For me, I do not even like to joke around about having a boyfriend on the side. That's a seed for suspicions and insecurity to blossom. Remember the principle of sowing and reaping.

Don't play with the enemy. You know when you are out of line with your comments or actions toward an outside person. Do not entertain foolishness! You can almost bet someone who is interested in you will approach you when you get into a committed relationship. Shut it down! You do not have to be rude about it, but firmly and confidently shut it down!

Your spouse cannot properly submit to you if there is a breach in trust, whether that breach is emotional, mental, physical, financial, and/or a spiritual. Trust is so delicate. It is easy to destroy, and hard to repair and regain after it has been lost. Without trust, there is no genuine intimacy. Be where you said you would be. Do what you said you would do. Tell the truth. Respect your spouse and behave how you would want your spouse to behave.

SEVEN

THE ART OF FLIRTATION

Believe it or not, not all men understand what it means to be romantic. Also, not all ideas of romance are the same. That's the importance of getting in tune with your hunny. Where one person may enter a house with rose petals on the floor and think how sweet and sensual the scene is, another may see the same rose petals scattered on the floor and wonder who is going to clean up the mess.

Describe your idea of romance:

_____

_____

_____

_____

_____

_____

_____

_____

What is his idea of romance?

_____

_____

_____

_____

_____

_____

_____

_____

_____

Pay attention to what may seem like the little things he likes in reference to you. Maybe he likes when you wear your hair a certain way or one of your many fragrances. Try to give him those little moments of pleasure often. If you are not naturally an everyday fashionable dresser, try to dress up for your man. If you are going out for date night, throw on something eye-catching. His eyes are going to be somewhere, so they might as will be on you!

Public displays of affection (PDA) can provide a sense of confidence and cohesiveness. It shows the world that you two are an item. I have heard stories of conservative ladies being embarrassed by their men giving them love taps on the booty in public. To each their own. Talk about what type of PDA you are comfortable with and the types of affection you prefer to keep private. Remember, we all come from various backgrounds, so being aware of your spouse's background is essential when learning what he likes and dislikes.

Study your mate to keep your mate. Observing and being in tune with your husband can be beneficial in your interactions with him. Be in tune with his body language. What does it look like your husband needs from you in that moment? Sex is wonderful, but do not forget to give him affection in other ways to ignite his masculine senses. Kiss your husband. Rub on his chest and arms to speak to his inner strength.

Foreplay is not limited to the physical intimacy *directly* before sex. Foreplay can be an all-day, year-round stimulating activity. From wedding bells to the time you wake up until the time you come together when the business affairs and household matters of the day are done, foreplay is used to heighten and prepare your mind and body for a sexual encounter. Even an oven has to preheat before you shove your food in there! Just like a bank, in order to make a withdrawal, there has to have been a deposit. So, make consistent deposits into each other. Knowing your spouse's love language will help you understand how to make those deposits.

Ladies, oh, ladies! Show him you missed him while he was gone. Give your husband something to be excited to come home to. Whether it is a flirtatious message, a sexy pic, or a simple, "I can't wait til you get here," build his excitement to come home.

How do you flirt with your husband?

_____

_____

_____

_____

_____

_____

_____

_____

_____

Does he get the clues or the gestures? If not, it is time to come to the table and talk about it. _____

Does he like it? _____

One simple turn-on that many men do not even realize is a turn-on for them is a smile. Think about it. A smile is a gesture that invites one to take a chance on approaching another being. It creates a warm, open environment. A smile shows someone you are interested in engaging in conversation that could lead to intimate growth and interactions. If a woman is not interested or attracted to a man, the grimace on her face typically says it all.

Are you still doing the things to keep your man that you were first doing to get your man? Is your man doing the same? If not, it is time to get back to them. Sometimes, men and women become complacent and stop doing those things we did to get our mate. That isn't cool and it's kind of deceptive if you really think about it. Wives, bring back the sexy night attire and shaved legs. Husbands, bring back the flowers sent to her job and the surprise romantic evenings.

> *"Most men are pretty simple. They want food, sex, attention, and affection." – C. Cason*

Wives, please sex your husband on the regular. I don't understand how a wife can be blessed with the opportunity to stay at home while her loving husband works, and still not give up the cookie! I would be more open than a 7-Eleven! Oh, yes, I said it. There is no way I would let my man be out there grinding and providing for his family, then come home and be forced to sleep his erection off. (Gots-to-be more careful!) Let me also say that being a wife is about much more than merely opening your legs for your husband. Sex is important in a marriage, but there is so much more to the role than sex.

If you read this and say, "But the quality of sex is trash." Well, that does not have to be the end of your story. It may be time to tap into some resources to stimulate your sexual interactions, and that extends beyond porn. From my perspective, porn can be a killer of realistic, meaningful sexual relationships between a husband and wife. Life happens. Pornography does not show the stretch marks a woman received from carrying a baby. They do not show the three to seven minutes of stamina the middle-aged man has in bed. It has great potential to create insecurities based on their portrayal of idealistic sexual experiences. Hebrews 13:4 tells us that the marriage bed is undefiled, so grab a book, visit a sex shop, and educate your minds!

Sad but true is the fact that Godly women are looked at as prudes when it comes to sexual relations within their marriage. I blame society and tradition for this view. People in the church approach sex like it's taboo unless they are preaching about the sin of fornication and adultery. What about those lessons regarding having a healthy, fulfilling sexual relationship with your husband? Or even a workshop about communicating your sexual needs and desires? I have seen less than a handful of those being offered and we need it. It amazed me to hear a man be shocked at the fact that a woman can have a relationship with Christ and love sex with her husband all at the same time. If men only knew that, when a wife feels loved right, she feels the need and desire to let out her inner freak!

I know the days can get busy, but be sure to give your mate the attention he needs, how he needs it. If you have to, put him on your to-do list, so you can have that reminder to "do" him. See what I did there? Save the energy to fulfill the *privilege* to care for him. Kids can be a roadblock or inspiration for creativity when it comes time to be sexually available for your husband. If your kids are not on a schedule for bedtime, maybe it is the time to establish one in your home. Some couples let their child or children sleep in the same bed with them. Personally, that would be a no for me and my house. This, in my opinion, makes sexually connecting with your husband more challenging. On the other side, if you decide to allow little ones to fall asleep in your bed, you two could slip away to another room for a little razzle dazzle.

Time Out

A phrase that really grinds my gears is, "You should like it when I (fill in the blank)." Well, why should I like (fill in the blank)? Because you like it or because your ex liked it? Either way, it is not fair to assume every person likes the same thing, especially in the bedroom. Men, and some women, may think they are doing something their mate likes, when in reality, he or she will keep quiet to avoid hurting the other's feelings. Now, this may sound harsh but it is the truth—ain't nobody got time for that!

Communicating about your particular sexual needs may be a challenging, uncomfortable conversation to have with your spouse. This takes a huge amount of security, trust, and courage. However, how can you improve the situation if you continue to keep your mouth shut? I hold strong to the premise of addressing your concern with the person it involves in order to give them the fair chance of acknowledging and possibly resolving the concern. It sucks knowing that our issues could have been resolved if someone simply took the courageous initiative to speak up and address the situation. They say closed mouths don't get fed. Communication can change the game though! Some things can be avoided before sexual action takes place if you communicate.

Listen to what your husband says he likes and process it. Learn what stimulates your spouse and try to meet him there. If you have questions, ask! Typically, no question is a stupid question. Ask if there is anything you could improve. Ask him if your hands are too dry and/or too rough when giving him a hand job.

Oral sex may be more of a sensitive topic. I know wives who do not like performing oral sex on their husbands although they like it performed on them. Then, there are wives who do not perform oral sex on their husbands because their husbands do not prefer it. Ask your husband if your mouth is wet enough for him during oral sex. Ask if there are specific areas on his penis that he would like you to concentrate and love on more. Ask if there is anything he would like to try during your time of sexually connecting. You may need to make a store run for lubricants, specially designed condoms, or props to enhance your bedroom experience. It is understood that most men do not like to ask for directions, so communicate with your spouse about your sexual likes and dislikes. Tell him when he turns you on and how he did it. Men love to hear when they have hit a spot on their wives' bodies that makes her cave. It boosts their sexual confidence. Strive to fill the other's sexual needs, so no one gets left out, and the experience is more pleasurable for both of you.

When we go into intimate conversations about sexual preferences, I advise all parties to go into it delicately until you understand the background, expectations, and even fears of your (potential) spouse.

We live in a world where it is important to keep in mind that you may not know if your loved one has experienced any type of sexual trauma, so please be sensitive. Ask if he likes anal stimulation. This is a question you should ask before sexual intimacy. Some men do not like their anuses touched during foreplay or sex because of traumatic experiences or because of the various connotations associated with it.

What turns your husband on?

_____

_____

_____

_____

_____

_____

_____

_____

_____

Do you like or enjoy doing what turns him on? Why or why not?

_____

_____

_____

_____

_____

_____

_____

_____

_____

Your mental state plays a major role when you and your husband are sexually connecting. First and foremost, it is important to like your husband. When you get to a point when you sincerely like where you and your husband are emotionally, the sex will be even better. And yes, your husband will notice a difference when y'all play "hide the snake." Sex should not feel like a chore, rather it should be a hobby, a fun one! It's an activity of intimacy that, hopefully, ends happily for you both. Now, you should not be making a mental grocery list or watching television or doing anything that prevents you from being physically, emotionally, and mentally present when y'all are engaging in sex. Simply turning off the TV can have a surprising effect on the emotional and sexual energy transmitted between you two. Depending on the mood you are intending to set, you may need to adjust variables in your environment.

Sexual intimacy should be an experience you both enjoy, at least, most of the time. I say most of the time because I understand there will be times when one spouse will not be in the mood or mindset to have sex, but that person will participate anyway. That's just part of putting your spouse's needs before your own. Please do not mistake me saying putting your spouse's needs before your own as something that is required to happen each and every time you are not in the mood for sex. When sex feels like a chore, something may need to be addressed immediately.

Anecdotally and maybe even scientifically, sex is more emotional for women than physical. However, we have to be careful not to be offended when our men do not want to make love every time. When we realize the kind of sex our partner needs at the time, we can better prepare our minds and emotions. Sometimes, men want to have competitive sex. Competitive sex includes both partners energetically performing at their best in order to cause the other to tap out. Competitive sex can be fun but very tiresome, so drink plenty of liquids. Then there is lazy sex. This is where one partner wants to do as little as possible to achieve an orgasm. Let's be real. Sometimes, men are going to want a quick release, then a nap. In the same respect, there are times when I just want to get off and go to sleep. NyQuil® has nothing on the natural sleep aid of an orgasm!

You need to know your limits as well. As sexy as some people think it seems, putting whipped cream in your genital area is a good way to get a yeast infection. Sugar does not pair well with dark, moist areas like the vagina. Be careful if you decide to use flavored lubricants. Some flavored lubes contain sugar which can cause irritation and infections. Yeast infections are no prize for good sex, so know your body and make adjustments as needed.

As you have been together for years and years, it may seem like you have done everything under the sun. Again, there is a plethora of free online resources to spark your creative side, such as Pinterest or Google. Find new ways to add and *keep* the spice in your relationship. It is good to keep him guessing about what you will do or wear next, in a good way, of course. Maintain *some* kind of mystery about yourself. Adding humor and laughter in the bedroom helps take the pressure of sexual perfection off both of you. Why does sexual intimacy have to be so serious all of the time? Why can't you get a laugh and a climatic release in the same encounter? Focus on enjoying your husband and the gift of sex God has given you two because as we get older, the natural hormones that once caused us to become aroused easily, decrease—making that gift a bit harder to open.

EIGHT

MAKING MY MARRIAGE A MASTERPIECE

You embark on a selfless journey of sharing and giving when you decide to get married. Your mentality must constantly remain in a mindset of "WE" and "US." Sometimes, we forget the sacrifice in loving someone. There is no love without sacrifice. That sacrifice includes putting aside temptations for the greater benefit and working of your relationship. If you are selfish and inconsiderate but you desire to be married, sincerely ask Jesus to change your heart. Be willing to do the work required to put that faith in action, because feelings will often come against accomplishing those goals and tests most certainly will come to measure your efforts. I know there have been times when I have had to push myself to cook because I wanted to make sure my man had a home-cooked meal. It is important to realize the ways your teammate is sacrificing, too.

A healthy relationship consists of a committed man and woman consistently serving each other in love (Galatians 5:13 NKJV). You should be making his load lighter through your nurturing spirit. Be grateful if your mate actually enjoys serving you, then return the gesture. Give until you cannot give anymore. Make serving your spouse fun for you. Seek Christ for ways to help your spouse. When we look to serve our spouses, we position ourselves to be blessed. In other words, we really do reap what we sow. Are you sowing things you want to reap? Sow bountifully to reap bountifully!

If what a queen does for her king out of love turns into a spectacle to stroke his ego, then she may be doing it for the wrong king. When you stop serving one another, that's a red flag, indicating love is being lost. An intentional course of action needs to be taken if you want, or don't want, to strengthen your relationship. There is a huge amount of sacrificing that goes into having a happy, fulfilling marriage. Imagine a husband and wife competing to *out-serve* the other in their marriage. The result will always be a win for both.

Teamwork Makes the Dream Work

Marriage will work if you work it and if you work together! The best and worst thing about men and women is that we tend to think so differently. That's a hard truth we must accept. I honestly think this was part of God's sense of humor. Then again, there may be a method to His madness.

Include your sweetheart in decisions you have to make. It is valuable to have his perspective, so get and utilize his insight. Remember, no good leader dominates all of the time. Good leaders analyze the facts, welcome the perspectives of their team, give credit where credit is due, and understand the principle, "When WE win, I win."

The person who is always getting what they want in a situation will rarely see anything wrong, which brings us to the subject of compromising. Compromising is a form of settling. That is really what it is. However, it is settling with a humble heart that says, I'm willing to give up my ideas and wants for a greater cause. It is this continual act of (here it goes again) *sacrificing* for each other that shows love and humility at its best. Take time to pray and meditate on the compromises that need to be made. Consider how the outcome will affect the other person. Be open to your spouse's ideas, and be willing to try their approach to an issue. If it works, give him accolades. If it does not, gently suggest your plan without saying, "I told you so."

Reflections/Prayer
How well do you and your husband compromise?

_____

_____

_____

_____

_____

_____

_____

What do you do when your ways are completely different?

_____

_____

_____

_____

_____

_____

_____

_____

Along with the ability to compromise, I believe *reciprocity* and *accountability* can make or break any relationship. Reciprocity is the continuous exchange of something. It typically benefits the person receiving the act of love, as well as the person initiating the act. We don't tend to correlate giving as a benefit to ourselves, since it causes us to sacrifice on our part. However, Proverbs 11:25 (NLT) states "If you refresh others, you will be refreshed yourself." I see why it's helpful to operate under The Golden Rule, meaning to treat others how you want to be treated, especially in intimate relationships. If you and your sweet thang are continually pouring into each other, no one will be empty. Once men and women understand and apply the law of reciprocity, relationships will become more pleasant, more fulfilling, and more beneficial to both parties involved.

Hold each other accountable for the standards you set in your marriage. Take notice of your self-awareness and emotional intelligence. Accept when you have made a mistake, though I know we ladies don't make mistakes, lol. Seriously, own up to your words, behaviors, and actions, even when they do not reflect you being your best self. Be willing to be patient when your husband works through your mistake in a different timeframe than you prefer. Again, men have feelings, too, and you have to respect his feelings.

Don't be mad when you have to do your part in your relationship. This goes deeper than your individual household chores. There is something in you that your spouse lacks. Whatever that thing is, let that be your love-offering to the relationship. If your spouse lacks financial knowledge, help your spouse grow in that area. If your spouse lacks emotional intelligence, approach him in love and correct him where necessary. Do your part! We grow from relationships by sharing experiences, perspectives, and knowledge. It is our responsibility to remain open and humble enough to extract the advice that could help us grow. Remember, you benefit from each other's strengths because you are a team. I am thankful to have a mate who challenges me in my weak areas. The challenges do not always feel good, but internally I know they are strengthening my character, and sharpening my iron. Continue to develop your own strengths so you can contribute to your team's success.

Evaluate your marriage and jot down two or three things you and your spouse bring to your marriage.

_____

_____

_____

_____

_____

_____

_____

_____

_____

_____

_____

_____

_____

_____

_____

_____

_____

_____

What are three goals you have for improving your role in your relationship this week?

_____

_____

_____

_____

_____

_____

_____

_____

_____

_____

_____

Checkpoint

If you have not taken *The Five Love Languages* quiz by Gary Chapman yet, I highly recommend you and your partner do so. The purpose of this quiz is to allow you to recognize what type of intimate activities you value. In turn, the results reflect how you like to be loved. Typically, the way one likes to be loved is how they show love to others. Share your results with him and take note of how your spouse likes to be loved. Philippians 2:3-4 (NLT) says to not be selfish, but take an interest in others, too. Once you discover your spouse's love language, you can focus on ways to shower him with love and appreciation in the manner he needs based on his desires, not your own.

As you are building, take an assessment on the condition and progress of your marriage often.

Consider these questions:

Are your needs being met?

Are you meeting your husband's needs?

Do you and your spouse need to review the expectations set in your relationship? Are there any adjustments that need to be made?

_____

_____

_____

_____

_____

_____

_____

_____

_____

_____

_____

_____

If you are unsure about any of the answers to the questions above, communicate with your man. You both must make conscious efforts to contribute (i.e. physical touch, cleaning the house, emotional support) to what your spouse values.

_____

Side note for Singles: If you are looking to get married, please be realistic about your expectations. I wish I could ask married women around the world whether or not marriage is the fairytale they thought it would be. But I guess that question can be answered by the alarming divorce statistics.

_____

Women, to help our men, say what you mean and mean what you say! We have our menfolk out here confused because we want them to figure out our riddles and emotions. Half of the time, we can't even figure out our own emotions. We say we don't want so-and-so, but get mad when he does not get us so-and-so. When did communication become a guessing game? Why do we make it so tricky? Why are we surprised when we don't get what we want when something completely different is communicated? Do yourself a favor. Do not expect your hunny to be a mind reader. This will end up disappointing you more than anything. Communicate your message as clearly and concisely as you can with no hidden inferences for the best results.

Remember to inform your husband first about the blessings and/or surprises that you experience. I think it is absolutely absurd for a spouse to post on social media, telling the world about something, before telling their own spouse. Informing your husband first, then the world (if need be), is indirectly letting him know where he is on your list of importance.

Never get tired of saying, thank you. You may say, "Well, my husband should know that I appreciate what he does." He may know, but what if he says, "Well, my wife should know I love her." You still want to hear I love you, right? The same goes for thank you.

You should be able to motivate each other, push

each other toward your passion and dreams. Speaking of which, you should communicate what those dreams and passions are. This is a conversation of intimacy, so expect to be closer after you share with one another. Even if you do not understand or agree with your spouse's purpose, try to understand it and ultimately respect it. Love is wanting the best for the other person. When your spouse is operating within their purpose, you will nine point eighty-nine times out of ten, see them being their best self.

> *Proverbs 17:22 (NKJV): "A merry heart does good, like medicine, but a broken spirit dries the bones."*

Having a sense of humor can drastically refresh your marriage. Take the time and ask yourself, and answer honestly, whether or not you have a sense of humor or is everything a matter of life and death. Are you too serious most of the time? Have you heard the saying, "Sometimes you have to laugh to keep from crying?" Oh, it is true! You have to laugh to keep from going batcrap crazy! It is a euphoric feeling when you and your love bunny can smile and laugh together. I ask myself how can I make my man smile today. I own my goofy, quirky personality. Whether it is a dance filled with intentional offbeat movements or it is being playful in a round or two of frisky wrestling, I don't mind doing corny things to make my man smile. People in relationships typically receive genuine joy from seeing their mate happy. Smile and laugh as often as you can because life has a natural way of bringing moments where you feel you cannot find a piece of joy to stand on or a reason to be hopeful. Choose JOY. Don't take yourself so seriously all the time. Loosen up, Gertrude! Do not lose your sense of playfulness, use it. It is this kind of light-heartedness that keeps you both energetic and youthful in spirit.

I cannot stress enough the importance of finding out what your husband likes and enjoys all the way around. It takes a broadening of your perspective to be in a relationship with anyone, a look outside of oneself. Understand we are all unique individuals with various interests and dislikes. Surprise him with things he enjoys, whether it is tickets to a sporting event, that fancy outdoor grill, a cologne he likes, or the tried-and-true morning sex. (Ladies, there is nothing wrong with making the first move. Men like to know they are sexually wanted, too.)

Name a few things your partner enjoys. (*This can include tangible things such as foods, gifts, hobbies, etc.*)

-
-
-
-
-
-

Consider learning the basics about the hobbies each of you enjoy. Not only does this tidbit of information give you more insight into who your spouse is, it also gives you gift ideas that will show you are mindful of the things each of you like to do. Try not to force your hobbies on your husband. This is different than introducing him to your hobbies and maybe even having him participate in them once to experience your hobby. Find something you both like to do and enjoy that common interest. In one former relationship, we liked softball, so we joined the same recreational softball team. In another relationship, we enjoyed poetry, so we went to local open mic nights.

It's cool for a couple to start or invest in things together. It can be as simple as starting a Netflix series and committing to watch it together. Get out and do something for someone else as a couple. There are many organizations and causes that require volunteer assistance. Be a blessing to others on purpose as a unit.

Not only does it help a cause, but it can be effective in drawing you closer together. You're blessed to be a blessing.

While doing something new is exciting and refreshing, sometimes doing something simple or nothing at all together is just as rejuvenating. It is the corny inside jokes, the 2 AM pillow talks, the walks, the wandering drives, and the shared meals—the "little things"—that make your marriage special. In the busyness of life, take time out together to just BE. It is critical to realize early that quantity time does not equate to quality time. Make time for each other on purpose and with the purpose of being fully present in that moment. Embrace the feeling of your spouse's skin next to yours. Take in their scent. Melt in the words of your conversation. Just BE. This helps with deepening your friendship within your marriage. There will come a time when the children, if you decided to raise any, are grown and on their own or your schedule frees up by other means. You want to be sure you have cultivated a relationship that looks forward to the time you can focus more on each other.

"You bring out the worst in each other, so you know what to work on." – J. Daniels

In life, it is crucial that you both remain teachable. Life will throw you challenges that will shake your world. If you are not careful, it can break your relationship. Somewhere in my twenties during meditation, I created my own acronym for L.I.F.E.— Little Incidences Forming Experience. Think about it. Every situation we encounter builds on what we have already learned and what we now have the opportunity to apply and see for ourselves.

Anniversaries also offer those opportunities because they give us the time to reflect on the beautiful moments and highlight growth in the relationship. They are proof that you can work it out and move forward together. They show people can improve if given the grace and time to do so. Anniversaries are a time we should celebrate the spouses we have evolved to be.

In what ways have you evolved since the beginning of your relationship?

_____

_____

_____

_____

_____

_____

_____

In what ways has your spouse grown?

_____

_____

_____

_____

_____

_____

_____

_____

_____

Marriage is a refining process for both of you. Your husband will bring out some ugly parts of you, and you will do the same. The moment you realize both of you have been your worst at times, yet you're still choosing to commit and love through it, you experience **grace** at its finest. When I think of some of my worst displays of emotions, I am embarrassed to my core. Apologizing did not seem to be enough and it did not minimize those feelings of humiliation. However, it did humble me to a point I have never experienced before. As horrible as I felt, I am grateful to reflect and remember I am not as "good" as I thought, and that I still need work within my heart.

Take a moment to praise God for the work He has done in you thus far.

The Lord has a way of getting our attention. If you need a wakeup call, the Lord is gracious enough to supply your need. It is my hope that it does not take a near-death experience for you to see your husband and marriage how you need to see them. Fix your heart on appreciating your spouse and your marriage. It is in a famine when we appreciate cereal for dinner. It is in a world of violence and social injustice when we appreciate safe returns. It is in chaotic times when we appreciate the simple things. At the end of this life, you <u>will</u> be held accountable for the kind of wife you chose to be. Will you have glorified Christ in your position? Or will you have shamed the title of wife? You have the power to make that choice.

May your heart be softened toward your husband.

Proverbs 31:29 (NKJV): "Many daughters have done well, but you excel them all."

FINAL THOUGHTS

As I stated in the Introduction, when I started writing this book, I was single. By the time I finished my final draft, I was married.

I appreciate and respect the individuals who told me that marriage is hard work. I did not go into marriage expecting a fairytale, but preparation made the transition a bit smoother. Transition, in itself, is challenging. Combining your physical resources, as well as getting on the same page with finances, living standards, emotional, spiritual, and sexual needs, is a challenge.

I made a conscious decision not to dedicate a specific section to address communication. Effective communication must take place in everything and at all times. Never ever underestimate the power of communication. You learn so much more when your mouth is closed and your ears and spirit are open. That is not to say neglect your own needs. I am walking with you to encourage a shift in your perspective. Since the only actions and behaviors we can truly change are our own, I am offering a proactive and reactive opportunity to improve and save your relationship.

I would advise anyone who believes they are called to marry, to engage in marriage counseling by a trusted, knowledgeable professional. Listen to the responses and the heart of your potential spouse. Then consider the costs. What would you be willing to contribute in order to have the marriage you both desire? Another important consideration is to identify the wife you *want* to be versus the wife you may *have* to be. You may *want* to be a soft, sensitive wife who would break her back to tend to her husband's every need, but you *have* to be a wife who is strong, unwilling to take any crap from the person your husband may be now due to his unhealed heart.

I also wrote this book to remind *future* me of the principles I have been taught by people who genuinely care about the health and success of my own marriage. If nothing in this book challenges you like it did me, then, as the old folks say, "Just keep living." As I experienced tribulations in my marriage while writing this book, I have had moments where I read my own words and received not only confirmation, but strength. I have lived these pages. I have also had times where I did not want to apply my own words to my life or my marriage. There were days when I put my pain on paper and trusted God that it would be used to help someone in the future, and that's just being real.

At the end of the day, the question remains, "How bad do you want it?" How bad do you want your marriage to succeed? How bad do you want to strive to better your relationship with your spouse? How bad is it that you can or cannot decide to try again? Growth comes with pain sometimes, but most of the time, it is truly worth it.

Whether it prompted a change in your attitude towards your husband, provoked you to work on your communication, or pressed you to redefine your expectations for marriage, I wholeheartedly pray something in this book inspired you to look inside and decide if single is really where you want to be.

WORDS OF WISDOM FOR RELATIONSHIPS

1. BE HUMBLE. Don't be afraid to apologize. Admit when you're wrong and when you don't know something.

2. COMMUNICATE. Text messaging is great but not for every situation. How a message is perceived and received may be quite different than what was intended. Talk. Weigh your words.

3. FORGIVE. No one is perfect. We're all human and make mistakes. Don't be blind though. If the same mistakes keep happening, you may need to examine new solutions.

4. COMMIT. If you believe in the person, fight for him/her. How many times have we given our attention and time to people who were not worth it?

5. BALANCE. Don't play the blame game. Wouldn't you rather be happy than always aiming to be right?

6. PROTECT. Don't post your relationship problems on social media. Why bring more issues into an already difficult situation? Instead, talk to someone you trust.

7. LOVE. Never get too angry that you refuse to say, I love you. I once read, "You never lose by loving, but you always lose by holding back."

AFFIRMATIONS FOR MY MARRIAGE

* *The enemy will not divide or destroy my marriage.*

* *I love my husband, and my husband loves me.*

* *My husband and I are stronger together. We are a team.*

* *Happiness and health are in my marriage.*

* *Though my husband and I may disagree sometimes, we both have our marriage's best interest at heart.*

* *I understand my words can either build or destroy my marriage. I choose to weigh my words and build my marriage.*

* *I will listen with understanding to my husband and be mindful of my responses, both verbally and physically.*

* *I will make myself available to serve my husband in the capacity he needs, and in doing so, my needs are met.*

* *I am a wife of integrity. Therefore, my vows, heart, desires, emotions, and body are my husband's only.*

* *I love, honor, and respect my husband both in person and in his absence.*

* *My husband is blessed because he is connected to me. I bring wisdom, love, healing, joy, and peace ON PURPOSE to our marriage.*

What are some affirmations you would add?

-
-
-
-
-
-

Side note for Singles: I encourage you to start a wife journal with all of the wisdom and insight people have shared with you about marriage. It will help you remember, study, and practice what you want to become—a wife.

From my personal wife journal:
I want a spouse who will enjoy life with me. Love GOD.
Live. Dance in the rain. Gaze at the stars. Love me. Watch
the planes take off & land. Simple. Play a prank on me.
Celebrate. Make me brownies. Skate with me. Laugh. Get
mad but still love me. Movies. Surprise me. Walk with
me. Make 2 AM Walmart & Waffle House trips with me.
Watch the sunrise. Karaoke. Love me. Gun range. Race
track. Pool, not swimming. Teach me to swim. Enlighten
me. Make me better.

Living abundantly doesn't mean having the most, but making the most of what you have.

What are the simple things you want for your marriage?

_____

_____

_____

_____

_____

What are the simple words that can change your marriage?

_____

_____

_____

_____

_____

_____

_____

SPECIAL ACKNOWLEDGMENTS

Thank you to my friends and family who have loved me enough to tell me what marriage is truly about.

Thank you to my spiritual mentors and prayer warriors for your words of wisdom and encouragement.

Thank you to my brothers and friends in Christ who shared their insights from the male perspective. Thank you for your transparency and for allowing me to learn from your experiences in order to help me and other couples.

Thank you, Momma and Daddy, for believing in me.

Last, but certainly not least, thank you to my boyfriend-turned fiancé-now husband for allowing the world to see us just as we are—imperfect humans uniting as one. Thank you for being a catalyst for my transformation.

CPSIA information can be obtained
at www.ICGtesting.com
Printed in the USA
BVHW050019180522
637236BV00013B/843